# PICKING

# LOSERS

**Written and Illustrated by Rich Paul**

ISBN 978-0692928394

# Contents

Foreword by Vinnie Perrone

Cartoons and Captions by Rich Paul

# FOREWORD

Schemers and dreamers. The needy. The tweedy. Jailbirds. Railbirds. Cheats and elites. Whiners. Diners. Louts. Touts. Wags . . .

Nags.

The racetrack coaxes every breed, teases every strand, tickles every hope: the thoroughbred owner coveting a Derby winner; the jockey, a daunting rush of wind; the trainer, a horse as a living flame; the breeder, a pedigreed sensation; the clocker, a shrieking stopwatch; the bettor, a life-changing score.

To every human kind, the track is a beckoning Valhalla, seeping riches, flaunting opportunity, promising it all. Players may exit a metaphorical mountain of rubble, busted but never broken. "The best thing in the world is a winning day at the races," the sagacity goes, "followed closely by a losing day at the races."

There's no place like the track: an oval world squarely unto itself, a sporting outcast, a gated anachronism. The horse in a time of hybrid cars? A scratchy public-address rendition of *A Call to the Post* in a time of iPods? Reins in a time of global-positioning systems? Win-place-show in a time of on-line poker?

Well, sure. The track has always paid off in contradiction. Horses race counter-clockwise in pursuit of time. Bettors ponder odds, hoping to get even. They call race-tampering a fix. Whispered tips are dubbed steam, the stuff that vanishes into thin air.

"Horse sense," W.C. Fields once cracked, "keeps horses from betting on what people do." Such pith might aid in suppressing truancy and mortgage defaults and beer-binging among racehorses, but it leaves them precious few tales to tell. Their two-legged devotees, alas, put their mouths where their money was.

The track is pregnant with stories: the 8 horse in the third race has a new bit today, trained like Secretariat with it; the 5 horse in the sixth had surgery to fix an entrapped epiglottis, whatever *that* is; the 2 horse in the ninth somehow ate a bushel of gummy bears before his last start.

And afterward: "That guy can't train Fido to bark." "Rider can't find his way with a roadmap." "Horse couldn't go fast if you put him in a truck."

Long before the motorcar, the racetrack moved folks from every sphere, and still they come. Moneyed elegance sits in open-air box seats, opera glasses dangling at the chest, raised pinky to a martini stem, heralding the classic conformation of a chestnut colt. Inside, across the dim, cavernous grandstand, wizened stumblebums in sole-less shoes and mismatched, Depression-era clothes spit on the floor, shred their tickets and toothlessly revile another sad ride by another sad rider.

These are the track's syncopated rhythms: dissonant, engaging, irrepressible. The trainer beats each dawn, shambles into a tottering, open-sided barn to teach and saddle and gallop and nurse and audition and otherwise steel his charges for The Race. Jockeys sweat and starve to make riding weight, navigate in weakened wooziness these monstrous, high-strung, unpredictable enigmas. They ought to wear body armor; instead, they don a feathery flak-jacket and a beanie-helmet, willingly risking it all for The Horse.

The sport can proclaim itself The Greatest Show on Turf only for its mane attraction. A marvel of nature's engineering, the racehorse takes three strides on pipe-cleaner legs to reach top speed, 40 mph, flaunting its gift of flight across dirt and mud and grass, through rain and snow and wind and desert heat in a graceful, daunting power-glide. Imagine an athletic endeavor whose principals never talk to the media, keep none of their winnings and foof in front of spectators.

Some horseplayers incorporate such action into their betting, note it in red ink on a program or in the Daily Racing Form, file it under "body language." Bettors may scarcely control their own impulses, but they're certain they can tell equine fortunes. Hence their mad rush to the races, in a smoking rattletrap with dashboard warning lights blinking like a NASA console, and the inevitable entreaty by the track announcer: "Will the owner of a rusty Buick Regal, license tag BET2WIN, please report to your vehicle at once. Your car is locked, and the engine's running."

Disclosures of this kind spark no murmur among the racing masses, only tacit understanding.

Certain oversights are common when one racing minute can change your life.

Players. Prayers. Riders. Chiders. On a roll. In the hole. Trainers. Campaigners. Owners. Donors. Plums. Bums. The chase. The race . .

A special place.

----Vinnie Perrone

Quick, go catch up with the vet and ask him if he lost his Rolex!

I had to appear before the judges this morning. First they fined me, then they suspended me. Then they grabbed me, held me down and shocked me with my battery!

No, I didn't say feed Bill. I said
PAY THE FEED BILL!

Mirror, mirror on the wall, who can hold them best of all?

Parking is five bucks. For another five bucks I'll tell you how to get to the racetrack!

I like horse racing much more than baseball. It's easier to sneak away from my office than it is from my wife!

You heard me. Go get some super glue!

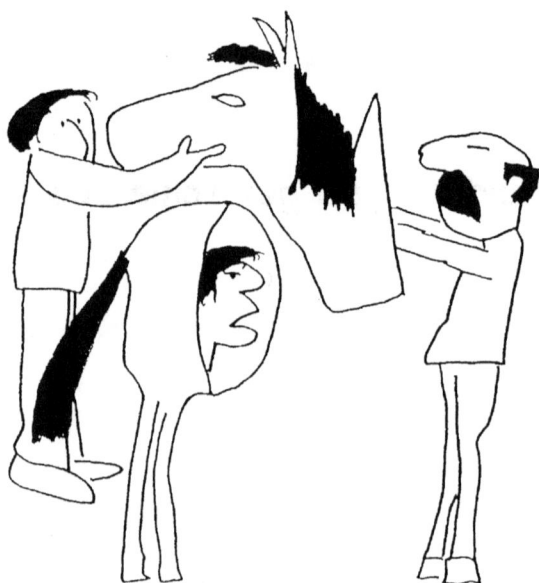

Oh yeah smart guy, what happens if somebody claims us?

He's been mixing what into the water?

The race goes in ten minutes and he's still fast asleep. Didn't I tell you two <u>not</u> to go out last night?

What's more important Johnny, your good name or your good health?

No, I don't use speed figures. I study their stool.

Forget him. He's got glue written all over him!

Now don't this beat all? I'm taking all this risk and I'm carrying a dead Double AA!

It's agreed. Everybody gets a share
of my 1-2-3 triple box!

Get up! You can't go back and run against maidens any more!

I can't tell which one is on top, but take a look at what the doc and nurse are doing in the back of the ambulance!

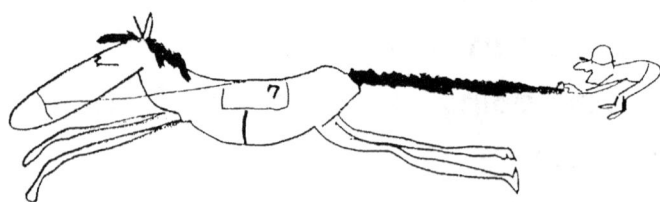

Hoo wee big fella! What are they smoking out back of your barn?

How many races are left until we
can start drinking?

You were so right. All I had to do was show him the gun and he did whatever I asked!

Yes sir, I tried to let you know you'd left without your change. I banged on this counter with my sponge!

Add this to the chart. One is lame, two is sore, three bled, four is dead, five refused, six ran away, seven bit his rider.

Who do they think they're fooling? They keep posting the same damn photo after every race!

Ladies and gentlemen, may I have your attention please. Please hold all tickets!

Wow, you finished that bottle in track record time!

Why get a table? Let's split a hot dog and bet more on doubles!

Hey, what's in this chili?

SECTION 8

Yeah, call it compulsive, but I only win when I go sit in the can!

Who told you it was okay to shoot jockeys during racing season?

You are THE worst. You rave about the one, tell Bill to bet the two, put your cash on the three and the four wins by a pole!

I'm just taking a deuce, so if you don't shut up I'll take your pants, too!

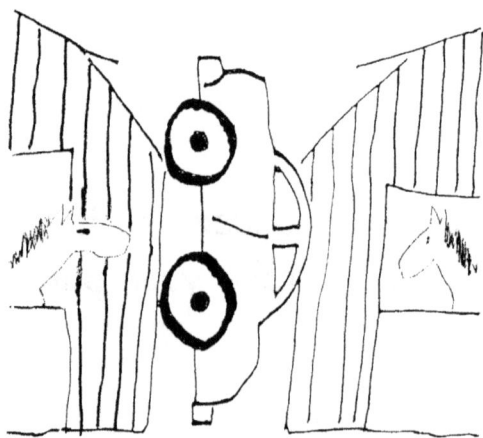

I told you I could get us a parking
spot on Big Cap Day!

Toto, I have a feeling we're not in Kansas any more!

And you can tell management we're not riding against monkeys!

Hey Richie Rich, you couldn't train Lassie to come home!

What do you think? I put springs in his shoes!

He's gonna ride at Aqueduct during the day and play for the Knicks at night!

Please Buddy, let me ride the big horse. Word of honor I've stopped the booze and the broads and the lying under oath!

Welcome back. I don't know anything about this race, either, and thank you to the many fans who have suggested I stop wearing underwear!

Oh my Lord, one more way to get killed at the races!

Hello, phone bet? Can I still get
down on the seventh?

One for us, one for them.

Twenty. Three. Four. Five. Here's
your hundred.

You're here and you're gonna drink!

Can you see where my money went?

There's an ugly mob outside, but they want to be sporting and give you a head start!

Our marketing department has determined that every time we raise the temperature inside the grandstand we sell more beer!

Sir, there is no smoking in this section!

I can't find a pulse, but he's still alive in the Pick 6.

My opinion? Man o War was juiced and Secretariat was pumped up on steroids!

Lucky lucky me! Every day my wife gives me money to get out of her hair and come out here and annoy you guys!

Why the long face?

What's this? I put in my cash and it spits out a bus ticket!

Stop beating a dead horse!

Excuse me, sir, are you leaving with your program?

I'm sick of losing my ass out here!

Look at the bright side. We can sell
your car and still make it back in
time to bet on the late double!

www.ingramcontent.com/pod-product-compliance
Lightning Source LLC
Chambersburg PA
CBHW061744020426
42331CB00006B/1350